AT RISK

TEST
PILOTS

BY
Jack C. Harris

CRESTWOOD HOUSE
New York

CIP

LIBRARY OF CONGRESS CATALOGING IN PUBLICATION DATA

Harris, Jack C.
  Test pilots.

  (At risk)
  Includes index.
  SUMMARY: Describes the training and job of a test pilot and
discusses the risks involved in this kind of occupation.
  1. Test pilots — Juvenile literature. 2. Airplanes — Flight testing —
Juvenile literature. [1. Test pilots. 2. Airplanes — Flight testing. 3.
Occupations.] I. Title. II. Series.
TL671.7.H34   1989   623.7'46048 — dc20   89-31126
ISBN 0-89686-429-4

PHOTO CREDITS

Cover: FPG International: Robert P. Morrison
Third Coast Stock Source: (John Nienhuis) 15, 16, 35;
    (Lawrence Ruggeri) 18; (Todd S. Dacquisto) 30
FPG International: 9, 11; (Robert P. Morrison) 4, 6, 25, 26,
    28, 37, 39; (Jim Howard) 23; (Philip Wallick) 33; (Marv
    Wolf) 36; (Dick Luria) 40
U.S. Air Force Photo released by Department of Defense: 42

Macmillan Publishing Company
866 Third Avenue
New York, NY 10022
Collier Macmillan Canada, Inc.

CRESTWOOD HOUSE

Produced by Carnival Enterprises
Printed in the United States of America
First Edition
10 9 8 7 6 5 4 3 2 1

TABLE OF CONTENTS

DANGER IN THE SKY

A roar rips through the air. You look skyward. High above, zooming through the clouds is a sleek plane. You watch the jet. But almost as suddenly as you heard it, it's gone. Soon, the jet is just a dot in the distance. Only its fading vapor trail is evidence of its passing.

For a moment, maybe you imagined yourself as the pilot of that jet. Maybe you felt your hands gripping the controls as you sliced the craft through the clouds. You felt the thundering jet engines. You felt that sinking sensation in your stomach as you dove and banked and lifted the jet higher.

If you can imagine these feelings, then you have an idea of what it's like to be a test pilot ...one of the brave men and women who take new jets into the skies before anyone else.

A new jet or plane begins as an idea. It's someone's dream for a faster, bigger, safer, or more powerful craft. For months or years, designers create the shape of the wings, and they improve the power of the engines. Models are built and tested. They're redesigned and tested again. Finally, the designers, draftsmen, and scientists feel that a new, full-size plane is ready to be built and flown.

Designers create new aircraft designs, scientists perfect the designs, and test pilots fly the new crafts for the very first time.

After many more months, a new craft is wheeled out of its hangar. It's ready to take to the air. The test pilot can now begin his tests. The pilot has been part of the project since the beginning. But now the test pilot and the plane have to work as one. The pilot has trained his mind and body to perfection. He's dressed in a special pressurized suit to protect himself from the high altitudes. A helmet shields his head. The radio in his helmet will keep him in touch with the anxious designers below. The pilot slips into the cockpit and lowers the Plexiglas canopy. He has a specific checklist with him. In radio contact with the tower controller, he checks each instrument.

He straps himself in. With a flip of a switch, the powerful engines scream behind him. The big jet rolls down the runway. Applying more and more pressure to the throttle, the pilot increases the speed. Faster and faster the jet zooms down the runway. As the pilot pulls back on his control, the aircraft leaps into the air.

Now the test begins. The test pilot maneuvers the jet *beyond* what it was designed to do. If he can fly it beyond its limits, then all the work that has gone into its design will have paid off. The pilot turns and banks and dives. He records the craft's performance and radios the report back to the tower.

Test pilots wear special suits to protect them from the pressure of high altitudes. This pilot is testing his suit.

Suddenly something goes wrong. The controls pull in the pilot's hands. The huge wings dip to the side. The ground seems to rush up toward the craft. Everything begins to spin.

"I'm having trouble," the pilot radios the tower. His voice is calm. His eyes dart across the controls, reading dials and instruments. Down on the ground the designers, draftsmen, and scientists huddle around the radio. They know if something is truly wrong with the plane's design, even the best pilot is in danger.

For long seconds there is silence. The people in the tower strain their eyes to see the jet. The only contact they have is the crackling radio signal.

In the plane, the pilot fights for control. He adjusts his speed. He realigns the wing flaps. He checks controls and dials on his panel. He seems to do a hundred things at once.

His skill pays off. With a rush of air, the plane levels off and screeches back toward the tower. "I'm stabilized," he radios back. "I'm back in control." The ground personnel cheer as the jet speeds by the tower. The pilot lowers the landing gear. Seconds later, the rubber tires touch the runway and the whine of the engine dies down. The test has been successful.

After their first flight in 1903, the Wright brothers continued to improve their aircraft. In this 1911 photograph, the Wright brothers test their newest design.

THE HISTORY OF THE TEST PILOT

Who was the first test pilot? Who was the first to risk leaving the safety of the ground for the unknown dangers of the sky? For the answer, we must go back through the history of aviation.

The ability to fly has been a dream of human beings ever since they looked up and saw the birds. Amazingly, however, the first official heavier-than-air flight didn't occur until Decem-

ber 17, 1903, near *Kitty Hawk,* North Carolina. It was there that *Orville* and *Wilbur Wright* made their historic 852-foot flight. It lasted just under a minute. Both brothers risked life and limb by flying that day. History records Orville was the first to pilot the craft. He was the world's first test pilot.

But Orville Wright was only the first pilot to test a heavier-than-air plane. Centuries before, 5th-century English monk *Roger Bacon* made the first form of actual "aircraft," the kite. The 16th-century artist and inventor *Leonardo da Vinci* made hundreds of aircraft design drawings. Da Vinci is credited with the creation of the propeller and the parachute. His drawings have shown designs for an ornithopter, a device that imitated the movement of birds' wings, a helicopter, and a glider. There is some evidence that da Vinci himself risked all by trying to fly in a crude glider. Perhaps Leonardo da Vinci was the world's first test pilot.

The "Father of Aviation" is considered by many to be *Sir George Cayley* (1773-1857). Cayley was a 19th-century British aeronautical engineer. His experiments with kites and gliders earned him the title.

Many inventors during the 19th-century concentrated on gliders and muscle-powered flight. Some of them got off the ground. But it is the

Many early inventors didn't want test pilots to try out their "flying machines." They wanted to fly the crafts themselves.

Wright brothers who are recognized the world over as the inventors of the first airplane.

There is a difference between test pilots of the past and test pilots of today. The inventors and test pilots of the past were one and the same. If people invented flying machines, it was usually because they desired the thrill of flight. They built the crafts so *they* could fly. The inventors wanted no one else to test their crafts before them. After the Wright brothers and the establishment of aircraft companies, however, people were employed as test pilots. The only requirements were bravery or, perhaps, foolhardiness.

Five years after his historic flight, Orville Wright was invited to show his plane to the U.S. Army. Carrying a passenger, he flew for more than an hour's time. A later flight for the Army resulted in a crash and the death of another passenger. However, with Wilbur's assistance, building plans went ahead. The U.S. Army Signal Corps bought the first military plane on August 2, 1908.

From that day on, more and more private aircraft companies appeared. Each one had its own test pilots. Most of the test pilots also worked as designers or members of the ground crew. Many were local heroes and were known as daring and fearless.

The outbreak of World War I meant advancements for aviation. Planes were needed for aerial attacks. Test pilots took even more risks as they became fighter pilots.

After the war, newer and faster planes were needed for passengers and cargo. Many firms offered large cash prizes for speedy planes. On May 20 and 21, 1927, American *Charles A. Lindbergh* challenged distance and hardship for 33½ hours. He became the first person to fly solo across the Atlantic Ocean in his *Spirit of St. Louis.*

During the 1930s, commercial air transportation expanded with *transcontinental* flights. With the coming of World War II, advancements came even faster as the defense of the United States became dependent on airplanes. After the war, the military's need for planes decreased. In 1945, commercial flights resumed after having been halted during the war. To meet this ever-increasing demand, more than 500,000 workers were employed by commercial aircraft manufacturers by the 1970s.

During these years, exploring space became a major interest. The task of testing new rockets fell to the test pilots. Men such as *Alan Shepard, John Glenn,* and *Neil Armstrong* became heroes by taking greater and greater risks. Alan Shepard became the first American in space. John Glenn was the first American in orbit. Neil Armstrong was the first man on the moon. Each one had begun as a test pilot.

Where will the future take us? What will the test pilots of tomorrow be asked to test? Planes will go faster than ever before. The future of aviation depends not only on progress and more advanced designs, but also on the daring and bravery of the test pilot.

THE DISASTERS

Every year, newspapers are filled with news of air disasters. In July 1986, a Boeing-377 cargo plane crashed onto a highway outside of Mexico City. The crash killed more than 40 people. In September 1985, 31 people were killed when a DC-9 crashed taking off from Milwaukee, Wisconsin. And on January 28, 1986, the *Challenger* space shuttle exploded on lift-off and killed all seven people aboard.

This list could go on back through the history of aviation. As bad as all these disasters were, each one taught important lessons. Each crash was investigated by experts to determine the cause. Many test pilots were members of these investigating teams. They know the statistics say that *half* of all air disasters are due to pilot or crew error. These trained pilots and technicians spend hours trying to learn what went wrong. They inspect wreckage fragments. The team listens to the recovered *flight recorder,* which is the "black box" that records cockpit conversation. Once the team determines a cause, the real work begins.

If the accident was indeed a crew error, new training sessions are set up to reeducate pilots. The pilots learn how they can prevent similar crashes in the future.

Sometimes the problem is a mechanical or design difficulty. Then it's back to the drawing board for the designers and engineers. They scrap the old design and build new ones. They install the new designs and call once again on the test pilot. The retesting of aircraft with new features is sometimes more dangerous than the original test flights. The test pilots know these planes *have* been involved in fatal crashes. The pilots must be extra careful when flying the redesigned planes.

Time is important, too. It takes time to reeducate pilots. If a mechanical failure was at

After an accident, test pilots fly the redesigned plane to make sure all problems have been corrected.

All new aircraft, whether they are commercial or military, are checked and rechecked. The test pilots and designers want to make sure the new craft are safe.

fault, other planes with the same mechanical features are grounded until the defect can be corrected.

Commercial airlines could lose millions of dollars in lost passenger service. Passengers are inconvenienced; there are fewer planes to choose from and reduced flight schedules. In the case of the military, air defense may be limited while defects are corrected. The test pilot's responsibilities extend to all these people.

These responsibilities add a great deal of pres-

16

sure to the test pilot's job. But it's this kind of stress, as well as the physical dangers, for which each test pilot is trained.

WHAT A TEST PILOT NEEDS TO KNOW

Men and women who have trained to be today's test pilots have studied and worked hard for years. In fact, the training of test pilots never ends. They must always know the latest technology. The training is hard. Those who love flying say it's worth all the effort.

Training to be a test pilot does have a beginning, however. Classes that can prepare a person for test piloting begin in junior high schools. Two important classes are math and science. When a test pilot is testing his plane, he has to record and report all the details of the flight. Since his reports have to include precise observations, the test pilot must be an expert in engineering and aeronautics. Math and science courses provide a good foundation for studying more difficult subjects.

More and more computers are being used to design, run, and test aircraft. A future test pilot needs to be knowledgeable about computers.

Even with the proper education, there is only one way to become a test pilot: by experience. Before becoming a test pilot, you first have to become a pilot. The requirements for becoming a pilot are different depending on what kind of pilot you want to be. The Army, Navy, and Air Force all have various requirements. The *Federal Aviation Administration* (F.A.A.), a section of the Department of Transportation, issues instructions regarding nonmilitary pilots.

Piloting skills are taught in many private piloting schools. But piloting can also be learned through the Civil Air Patrol, a branch of the military, or certain colleges.

Test pilots first must become pilots. They must be able to fly all kinds of aircraft.

Test pilot schools are difficult. A student's time is filled with flying instruction and course study. Courses usually last six months and include aerodynamics, math, and physics. More than half of those entering test pilot schools drop out. Sometimes they cannot keep up with the studies. Sometimes they cannot keep up with the physical requirements needed for this exciting but tough and dangerous job.

WHAT A TEST PILOT NEEDS TO DO

Along with studying, trainees must pass certain physical requirements. These tough requirements do not leave out women. Each year more and more women are becoming test pilots. They have proven they can act and react as fast as or better than male trainees.

But not just *anyone* can become a test pilot. Not even a straight-A student can become a test pilot based on his or her knowledge alone. Those students also have to be in good physical condition.

Newly designed aircraft are tested for speed and endurance. At the same time, the test pilot is examined to see if human beings can stand the pressures and speeds within the craft. A plane that cannot carry a pilot or passengers safely has to be redesigned. The test pilots need to be in condition so they can overcome the dangers and bring the plane and themselves safely back to the earth. If the test pilots need to eject, they must be able to control their parachutes and withstand the shock of descent.

A daily exercise routine and good eating habits help keep test pilots in good health. Such physical programs are a lifetime commitment. Test pilots have to *remain* in top shape all through their careers.

Someone in good physical condition also has an easier time handling the daily studies and training. All test piloting schools include tough physical training classes. Many students drop out from these classes because they can't keep up. If the students cannot maintain the physical pace, they could be a danger to themselves. They could also be a danger to their own flight crews and the aircraft.

Some branches of the military publish diet and physical training manuals. These manuals outline the programs recommended to their test pilots. They are available in libraries or local recruiting offices.

Some physical difficulties cannot be overcome

by diet and exercise. For instance, people who have vision or hearing problems may not be able to meet test pilot requirements. Colorblind people cannot be licensed as pilots in many places.

Each potential pilot has to be fit in both mind and body. The physical and emotional requirements needed for dangerous takeoffs, maneuvers, and landings are extremely strenuous. If someone cannot meet these standards, he or she should choose a different profession.

FLIGHT TRAINING

In addition to mental and physical training, a test pilot participates in flight training. Much of this training is done today in *flight simulators.* These are nonflying, full-sized mock-ups of aircraft cockpits. Computers turn and twist the simulators as if they are being blown by winds and weather. Projectors and tapes recreate actual flight situations. Trainees sitting inside a simulator see and hear as well as feel what a real flight is like.

The computers create disasters and dangers the trainees have to face. Even though they know it's all fake, the realism created by the simulators soon makes the trainees forget that none of it is real. The reactions many trainees have inside the simulators prove they actually believe they are in life-and-death situations.

Actual flight time is included in some military test pilot schools, but only on aircraft that already have been tested. No trainee actually *tests* an untried air vehicle.

A test pilot school only prepares the students for what they will do when they become test pilots. To actually *be* a test pilot is a different matter. Before the trainees can be considered real test pilots, they must actually test aircraft under exacting field conditions. The successful students go on to be the men and women known as test pilots.

ASTRONAUTS ARE TEST PILOTS

When scientists wanted to explore outer space, they turned to test pilots to find their astronauts. In 1958, the *National Aeronautics and Space Administration* (NASA) chose seven test pilots. These pilots were trained as astronauts for Projects Mercury, Gemini, and Apollo.

At the time, little was known about the dangers of space. No one was certain of the risks.

Test pilot trainees ride in flight simulators to recreate actual flying situations.

23

Scientists didn't know the effects of weightlessness. They weren't sure if a human being could stand the thrust needed for a rocket to escape the pull of Earth's gravity. They did know, however, that test pilots would have the strength and bravery to withstand these limits.

At first, requirements for test pilots who wanted to train as astronauts were: U.S. citizenship, excellent physical condition, a height of up to six feet, a B.S. degree in engineering or science, and at least 1,000 hours of jet aircraft flying time or graduation from a military test pilot school.

In later years, NASA made other categories for astronauts who were not test pilots. However, each of these new trainees had to pass the same tough requirements as the test pilots.

Once chosen, astronauts receive two areas of specific training. The general or overall training includes classroom instruction and physical training.

After an astronaut is assigned to a specific flight, a second series of training begins. This next series prepares the astronaut for the specific mission of his or her flight. These training sessions might last six months or more. During this time astronauts use flight simulators to get a "feel" for what a real space flight will be like. At the same time, an entire back-up crew is trained with the astronauts. If any member of the primary crew has to drop out of the program, a back-up crew member is ready to take his place.

Just as the test pilot reports on the performance of his aircraft, the astronaut communicates the information gathered on a space flight. This data might be about the operation of the spacecraft or about a specific mission. Astronauts, like test pilots, must be able to accurately report information to the ground crew.

In recent years, many daring people have trained for careers as astronauts rather than just test pilots. But even with that goal, students still

Some of the astronauts on the Space Shuttle Columbia *may have started their careers as test pilots.*

The ejection seat is one of the safety features that test pilots must try out and approve.

have to go through test pilot training before they can even *begin* to be considered as possible astronauts.

OVERCOMING THE DANGERS

Being a test pilot is dangerous. Test pilots know they are taking chances. But one of the reasons they *are* test pilots is to help make aircraft safer. One of their goals is to help get rid of air disasters. That's why test pilots also test safety features.

In a military plane, pilot safety is the first concern. In a commercial flight, passenger safety comes first. Different safety features are used when the craft is taking off and when it is in flight. Other safety features are used when it's landing and when it has come to a stop. It is the pilot's job to know which device to use under which circumstance. The test pilot makes sure all safety devices work. Many times it is the test pilot who suggests a safety feature. Other times, a new safety device is designed and tested because of an actual disaster.

Ejector seats, inflatable safety escape chutes, and rafts are always being redesigned and tested. Just as a plane's performance can only be truly tested during a real flight, safety equipment can only be proven in an actual disaster. Testing techniques have become more and more exact. But only a real crash or a real need to eject can show if all safety measures taken are enough.

And what about the future? Tomorrow's aircraft are going to be designed for faster travel. New safety devices will be created and tested. If future commercial flights include space flight, then passenger safety in space will have to be considered. What designs will be necessary in space where there is no gravity? What features will be needed to ensure a safe return?

After the *Challenger* space shuttle disaster in 1986, the cockpit was redesigned. The shuttle's cockpit can now be blasted away from the huge fuel tanks. It can parachute safely to Earth. Similar separating cockpits and passenger areas are being tested for commercial and private airplanes as well.

One of the newest advances is an electronic anticollision device. In March 1987, the first device was tested not by a test pilot, but by a commercial pilot on a regular commercial flight.

The ground crew demonstrates how they would rescue a test pilot from a failed aircraft.

The device transmits radar signals. The signals are bounced back when they encounter other flying aircraft. The bounced-back signal shows the other aircraft's position and *altitude* on a screen in the cockpit of the original plane. If the other aircraft is too close, a warning signal sounds.

All of these safety devices have been or will be tested by test pilots. The test pilots know that if safety devices don't work, then their lives, and the lives of the people the devices are designed for, are in danger.

WOMEN TEST PILOTS

Years ago, many thought only men could be test pilots. But early on, daring young women took to the skies. They proved they were just as capable as men. One of the most famous female aviators was *Amelia Earhart* (1898-1937). She was the fist woman passenger on a transatlantic flight. In 1932 she became the first woman to make a solo Atlantic flight.

In 1935 Earhart became the first woman to fly the Pacific Ocean. Later that same year, she set a speed record flying from Mexico City to New York. She vanished in July 1937 while attempting an around-the-world flight. Her deter-

mination led to widespread acceptance of women as fliers.

In the 1970s, NASA's astronaut program invited women to join. A number of American women have traveled in space since then. In 1984, *Sally Ride* became the first female space shuttle astronaut when she flew aboard the *Challenger.*

Today, with male and female roles becoming more equal, the number of women test pilots is increasing. In fact, some studies show a woman's average reaction time may, in some cases, be faster and more accurate than a man's. Each year, women are more and more involved in the dangerous and exciting role of test pilot.

WHY BECOME A TEST PILOT?

Why would anyone want to be a test pilot in the first place? Test piloting is probably one of the most dangerous jobs in the world. Often, test pilots are involved in top-secret projects for the military. Some projects are so confidential test pilots are not allowed to talk about them to anyone, not even their families.

Since their jobs are so filled with peril and

A test pilot trainee runs through a preflight check as his instructor watches closely.

risk, they can't buy life insurance. The hours are long and hard. The training and study to become a test pilot are difficult. Why, then, would anyone want to go through so much hardship?

Quite often, these reasons are the same ones test pilots give for *becoming* what they are. They *know* the job is dangerous, but danger also means excitement. These men and women love the thrill of flight. They love the exhilaration of height and the sensation of speed. These emotions overcome the elements of danger for these daring people.

Since the job is treacherous, it also pays well. While military test pilots might not earn as much money as commercial pilots, they are involved in many more projects. Test pilots tend to retire early, but their experience in the air is a valuable asset for aircraft manufacturers.

And, even if they can't talk about their specific missions, test pilots are still highly respected. People realize the risks they take and admire them for their daring, their courage, and their knowledge of a space-age skill.

Test pilots love the thrill of flight and the excitement of testing new aircraft.

A DAY IN THE LIFE
OF A TEST PILOT

A *typical* day in the life of a test pilot is un-eventful. The day begins with breakfast and exercise followed by a review of the day's schedule. There are meetings with scientists and designers. Some of these meetings may be over lunch, across drafting tables filled with blueprints and computer print-outs.

A test pilot might spend the afternoon checking his equipment. He checks for leaks in his pressure suit. He makes sure his helmet radio is working properly. Late afternoon may be filled

with preparations for future flights or reviews of past flights. A typical day in a test pilot's life may not be filled with danger at all.

But eventually, a flight is scheduled. While test pilots must be ready at all times, they usually work in a rotation. For two days out of every eight, they are flight ready. That means they're ready to board a plane at a moment's notice. The other six days are spent in planning, training, and study sessions.

On a flight day, the test pilot eats well. He has spent the previous day planning for the test flight. The last thing he does before suiting up is to make a final check of the weather. Meeting with his ground crew and flight crew, he also makes a final check of every aspect of the aircraft to be tested. The test pilot carefully records the time, date, weather, and winds. The runway length is noted as well as its temperature. The fuel weight and the overall weight of the aircraft are logged in.

The wing flaps, gears, cargo doors, and engine are all given a final check. The pilot, copilot, flight mechanic, and all official observers log in. Then the flight crew goes over the specific tests to be made during this flight. No aircraft is tested just once. Each aircraft is tested over and over again so every part of the perform-

To prepare for upcoming flights, test pilots carefully review past test flights.

The ground crew and test pilot check all equipment before a flight. Once the craft passes these preflight checks, it is ready for more demanding tests.

ance can be completely checked. There are tests for flight control, speed, distance, and instrument performance.

Once the test pilot and crew have finished their ground tests, the pilot climbs into the cockpit. The jet roars into the air.

The *calibration* or *instrument test* is first. This test checks the accuracy of the instruments, and is run first since all other tests depend on the accuracy of the instruments. Early morning, between 4 and 5 A.M., is the best time for this kind of test because the air is calm.

During the pacer test, the new craft is flown in formation with a tested plane. The pilots make sure the instruments of both planes match.

Airspeed is measured during the *pacer test*. The new aircraft is flown in formation with a pacer plane. The pacer plane's instruments have already been checked for accuracy. The airspeed can also be checked by the *tower flyby test*. In this test, ground crew members with ground speed indicators measure the plane as it roars by. If all the indicators match, the new plane passes the test.

The *level flight acceleration test* is an exciting and dangerous test. The craft is flown straight and level, then the pilot slows down to the very minimum speed. One slight error and the engines could stall out and the plane would fall helplessly to Earth.

Once the pilot slows down as much as he dares, he *accelerates* to the plane's maximum speed. He streaks across the sky in front of a deafening roar. The pilot levels off to a different altitude and tests the plane again. A camera records the instrument panel at five-to-ten second intervals. At each altitude, speed, temperature, and fuel consumption are checked.

The *check climb test* might be next. The pilot noses the craft upwards to see how fast and how far the plane can climb into the heavens.

During all tests, the test pilot is constantly aware of changes going on around him. Most changes are clearly indicated on his control panel, but some are just "felt" by the pilot. His instincts fed by his experience will tell him if the aircraft is flying properly. If not, his skills will have to come into play. He will be forced to use his skills to guide the plane safely to land. One small lapse of memory could mean a crash.

When the tests are complete, successful or otherwise, the pilot and his crew land and disembark. They are checked physically by a doctor, then head to debriefing. Checkpoint by checkpoint, the test pilot and crew go over every part of the test with the ground crew. Any

38

After all tests are completed, the test pilot lands the new aircraft and records the data for the designers and scientists.

problems are noted and examined in detail the next day.

For now, the test pilot's work is done. He gets out of his flight suit and heads for the showers and a good night's rest. Once the tests are completed successfully, there may be time for a celebration.

All of these controls must be tested by a test pilot before anyone else flies the plane, and sometimes that testing can take a long time!

TRAINING THE TEST PILOTS OF TOMORROW

What will training be like in the world of the future? It might be less dangerous in some areas, more so in others. Today training exercises on simulators are more realistic than ever. But tomorrow might provide mock flights that are even more realistic. Computer graphics are getting better each day. Improved computers may someday provide trainees with three-dimensional images that even their trained eyes can't tell from reality.

Simulations based on video games are being used to train pilots. If you're a video champion, you may have the talent to become a test pilot.

Scientists are working with computer chip implants. The implants allow the human brain to be directly linked with a computer. Tomorrow's test pilot trainees may actually be linked mentally with their simulators, making turns and increasing speed by the power of thought alone.

The entire history of heavier-than-air flight has occurred in the 20th century. If we can advance so much in less than 100 years, just think what we'll be able to accomplish in the next ten decades!

THE PLANES OF THE FUTURE

What kind of planes will the test pilots of tomorrow be testing? Some will be secret aircraft such as the stealth bomber. The bomber is reported to be invisible to all detection equipment. Others will be like the fabled *X-15*. Still other planes of the future will be powered by atomic

fuel and solar energy. They will be faster and safer than any aircraft known today.

Planes of the future may not even have wings. They may be powered by magnetic forces. They'll be propelled by the movement of the earth, sun, and moon. These aircraft will have to be tested. Robot pilots might test early aircraft models. But eventually, after every precaution has been made, a human being will take the controls. A human being will pilot the craft across the skies at perhaps undreamed of speed. These people will build on the foundation established by past brave men and women. They will face the dangers and take the risks in the name of progress. And they will still be called . . . test pilots.

The stealth bomber is only one of the many new aircraft that will be flown by test pilots of the future.

FOR MORE INFORMATION

For more information about test pilots, write to:

Air Force, Office of Air History
HQ, USAF/CHO
Building 5681
Bolling Air Force Base
Washington, DC 20332-6098

Federal Aviation Administration
    Technical Center
ACT 624
Atlantic City Airport
Atlantic City, NJ 08505

American Institute of Aeronautics
    and Astronautics
Technical Information Service
557 West 57th Street
New York, NY 10019

National Aeronautics & Space Administration
News and Information Office,
    Public Affairs Division
400 Maryland Ave. SW
Washington, DC 20546

44

GLOSSARY/INDEX

Accelerate 38—To increase the speed of an aircraft.

Altitude 29, 38—How high an aircraft is flying, measured in feet above sea level.

Armstrong, Neil 13—The first man on the moon.

Bacon, Roger 10—English monk who invented the kite.

Calibration test 36—Also called an instrument test. This test checks the accuracy of an aircraft's instruments. This test must be done first because all other tests depend on the accuracy of the instruments.

Cayley, Sir George 10—British inventor whose experiments with kites and gliders earned him the title "The Father of Aviation."

Challenger 14, 28, 31—The space shuttle that exploded in January 1986.

Check climb test 38—In this test, a pilot flies the aircraft upwards to see how fast and how far the plane can climb.

da Vinci, Leonardo 10—Italian artist and inventor; creator of the ornithopter and the parachute.

Earhart, Amelia 29—First renowned female aviator.

Federal Aviation Administration 18—The

GLOSSARY/INDEX

F.A.A.; the government agency responsible for setting pilot standards.

Flight recorder 14—The "black box" that automatically records cockpit conversation.

Flight simulator 21, 23, 24, 40—A computer-driven device that creates flight conditions for test pilot trainees.

Glenn, John 13—The first American astronaut to orbit the Earth.

Kitty Hawk 10—North Carolina site for the first heavier-than-air flight by Orville and Wilbur Wright.

Lindbergh, Charles A. 12—The first man to fly the Atlantic solo; piloted *The Spirit of St. Louis.*

Level flight acceleration test 37—In this test, a pilot flies the aircraft at different altitudes. At each altitude, speed, temperature, and fuel use are checked.

National Aeronautics and Space Administration (NASA) 22, 24, 31—The agency responsible for the U.S. space exploration efforts.

Pacer test 37—This test measures the airspeed of an aircraft. A new aircraft is flown next to a pacer plane (the pacer's instruments have already been tested). While the two planes are

GLOSSARY/INDEX

flying, the instruments of each plane are compared. If the readings match, the new aircraft passes.

Ride, Sally 31—America's first female space shuttle astronaut.

Shepard, Alan 13—The first American in space.

Spirit of St. Louis 13—The aircraft piloted by Charles A. Lindbergh on his solo flight across the Atlantic.

Tower flyby test 37—This test, like the pacer test, measures airspeed. The tower flyby test is conducted by the ground crew who use instruments to test the aircraft as it flies by.

Transcontinental 13—An aviation term referring to crossing an entire continent.

Wright, Orville 10, 12—The pilot and co-inventor of the first heavier-than-air plane and brother of Wilbur Wright.

Wright, Wilbur 10—Co-inventor of the first heavier-than-air plane and brother of Orville Wright.

X-15 41—Experimental aircraft.